EDGE BOOKS™

TOP SECRET FILES

SECRETS OF THE U.S. CIVIL WAR

BY LINDA LeBOUTILLIER

CAPSTONE PRESS
a capstone imprint

Edge Books are published by Capstone Press
1710 Roe Crest Drive, North Mankato, Minnesota 56003
www.mycapstone.com

Library of Congress Cataloging-in-Publication Data
Names: LeBoutillier, Linda, author.
Title: Secrets of the U.S. Civil War / by Linda LeBoutillier.
Description: North Mankato, Minnesota : Capstone Press, [2017] | Series: Edge
   books. Top secret files | Includes bibliographical references and index. |
   Audience: Ages 8-14.
Identifiers: LCCN 2016039224| ISBN 9781515741381 (library binding) | ISBN
   9781515741428 (pbk.) | ISBN 9781515741602 (ebook : .pdf)
Subjects: LCSH: United States—History—Civil War, 1861-1865—Secret
   service—Juvenile literature. | United States—History—Civil War,
   1861-1865--Equipment and supplies—Juvenile literature. | Spies—United
   States—History—19th century—Juvenile literature. | Spies—Confederate
   States of America—Juvenile literature.
Classification: LCC E608 .L43 2017 | DDC 973.3/85--dc23
LC record available at https://lccn.loc.gov/2016039224

Editorial Credits
Nate LeBoutillier, editor; Steve Mead, designer;
Pam Mitsakos, media researcher; Laura Manthe, production specialist

Media Credits

Alamy: GL Archive, 7; Bridgeman Images: Pictures from History, 12; Getty Images: Bet-
tmann 10 top left, 14, Culture Club, 17; iStockphoto: Maxim Anisimov, 25, 27; Newscom:
akg-images, 20-21, Liszt Collection Heritage Images, 8, Mathew Brady Picture History,
10 bottom right; North Wind Picture Archives: Maryann Groves, 11, North Wind Picture
Archives, cover, 15, 19, 28; Shutterstock: Billion Photos, 5, Everett Historical, 6, 13, 22, 24,
26, Karyl Miller, 2-3 background, L.E.MORMILE, 16 bottom right, Morphart Creation, 18,
Robert B. Miller, 16 bottom left; Wikimedia: Wikimedia, 9; Wikipedia: Wikipedia, 23

Shutterstock: Design Elements, Davor Ratkovic, Everett Historical, javarman,
STILLFX

Printed and bound in the United States of America.
010081S17

TABLE OF CONTENTS

A LITTLE GIRL'S DIARY

Carrie Berry lived in Atlanta, Georgia. She was six years old when the Civil War broke out on April 12, 1861, between the northern states—the **Union**—and the southern states—the **Confederacy**.

Two days before her 10th birthday, Carrie began a diary. On her birthday, August 3, 1864, she wrote: *This was my birthday. I was ten years old, But I did not have a cake; times were too hard so I celebrated with ironing. I hope by my next birthday we will have peace in our land so that I can have a nice dinner.*

Atlanta surrendered to the Union one month after Carrie's birthday, on September 2, 1864, but Southern people continued to live there. In November the Union decided to set fire to factories, warehouses, and railroad stations in Atlanta. About 1,600 people still lived in the city. They were afraid their houses would burn down, and some houses did. On November 15, Carrie wrote: *This has ben a dreadful day. Things have ben burning all around us. We dread to night because we do not know what moment that they will set our house on fire.*

Fortunately, Carrie's house did not burn down. The Civil War ended on May 9, 1865, before her 11th birthday. She got her wish for peace.

Union—the United States of America; also the northern states that fought against the southern states in the Civil War

Confederacy—the southern states that fought against the northern states in the Civil War; also called the Confederate States of America

CHAPTER ONE

THE PEOPLE WHO FOUGHT

The Civil War drew many people into service. Some, like Confederate general Robert E. Lee and Union general Ulysses S. Grant, became famous. Many others did not, though they still played big roles in the Civil War.

MANY LANGUAGES

Many soldiers who fought in the Civil War were not born in the United States. About one in every five Union soldiers—and one in twenty Confederate soldiers—were **immigrants**. They spoke many different languages. One Union regiment was made up of soldiers and officers who spoke 15 languages. Major General Franz Sigel gave orders in German. The orders were translated into Hungarian for his officers. Then they were translated into English for the rest of the men.

Major General Franz Sigel →

WOMEN SOLDIERS

Up to 400 women sneaked into the Union and Confederate armies. Some joined along with their husbands. Many were farmers' wives and daughters who were used to hard work. Uniforms were heavy and didn't fit well, which helped to disguise women's curves. Soldiers slept in their clothes and rarely bathed together. Women who were discovered were sent home, imprisoned, or even put in mental hospitals. Many were never discovered.

FIGHTING FACT

Sarah Edmonds Seelye was known as Franklin Flint Thompson in the Union Army. She was the only woman given a veteran's **pension** after the war.

↑ Francis Clalin Clayton, female Civil War soldier

immigrant—a person who comes to live in a different country than the one in which they were born

pension—money the government sends to retired people

THE NAME'S BOND, ELLEN BOND

Many southerners didn't think of slaves as people, much less spies. Most slaves were not sent to school. A number of southerners assumed that many slaves were not smart enough to read.

Mary Elizabeth Bowser was a slave in Virginia. Before the war, the Van Lew family freed her and her family. Bowser stayed on as a servant. Mrs. Van Lew, noting Bowser's intelligence, sent her to school. When the war started, Bowser was asked to be a spy for the Union. She would work in the household of Confederate President Jefferson Davis.

↑ Jefferson Davis residence, Richmond, Virginia, 1865

Bowser pretended to be a slow-witted slave who was named Ellen Bond. People nicknamed her "Crazy Bet." President Davis discussed war plans in front of her. He left papers on his desk when she was cleaning his office. Not only could Bowser read, she had a photographic memory. She could repeat word-for-word everything she read on Davis' desk. She gave information to another black spy who drove a delivery wagon. When Bowser was discovered, she ran away.

A SHIP'S PILOT AND POLITICIAN

Robert Smalls, a slave, was a pilot of the C.S.S. *Planter,* a Confederate ship. One night when his white captain and first mate were ashore, Smalls sailed the ship out of the harbor and surrendered it to the Union. After the war Smalls was elected to the U.S. House of Representatives from the state of South Carolina.

THE YOUNGEST SOLDIER

Many soldiers on both sides of the Civil War were children. The youngest soldier in the war was Johnny Clem. He joined the 22nd Michigan unit as a drummer at the age of nine. The other soldiers in his unit gave him money until he was added to the payroll. He served in the U.S. Army for 43 years, longer than any other Civil War veteran. His grave is in Arlington Cemetery.

↑ Johnny Clem

AMERICAN INDIAN AUTHOR

General Ely S. Parker, a lawyer from the Seneca tribe, authored the Articles of Surrender, the written agreement that ended the war. Robert E. Lee, the South's main general, said, "I'm glad to see one real American here." Parker replied, "We are all Americans."

NATIVE AMERICANS WHO FOUGHT

American Indian tribes fought on both sides during the war, but the Cherokee, Chickasaw, Choctaw, Creek, and Seminole Indians fought for the South. The Confederacy agreed to pay their tribes money. They also promised the American Indians representation in the government. After the war the land of all the tribes that supported the South was taken away from them as punishment by the government of the United States.

Most Cherokee soldiers switched sides during the war to join the Union. One Cherokee chief remained loyal to the South. Brigadier General Stand Watie did not want to accept defeat and refused to surrender until a month after the war ended.

General Stand Watie →

CHANG AND ENG

↑ Chang and Eng Bunker

In 1839 Chang and Eng Bunker came to America from Thailand, called Siam at that time. They were American citizens when the war started. Although they were Confederate supporters, Eng was drafted to fight in the Union army. But that wasn't the main problem. Chang and Eng were **conjoined twins**. They were the original "Siamese twins." One couldn't go without the other. Neither one fought, but their sons did—for the South.

PROBLEMS WITH UNIFORMS

When the war started, there were not enough uniforms for the Union army, and there weren't any standard uniforms for the Confederates. Soldiers on both sides wore state militia uniforms or just **civilian** clothes from home. This made it hard to tell which side a soldier was fighting for. As a result, many soldiers were killed by friendly fire. Union army uniforms were standardized, or made the same for everyone, in 1862. Confederates standardized their uniforms in 1863.

FIGHTING FACT

A great-great-granddaughter of Chang Bunker won the 2013 Pulitzer Prize for music. Caroline Shaw became the prize's youngest recipient, winning at age 30.

↑ Union volunteer soldiers of the 31st Pennsylvania Infantry and the family of one of the soldiers

FIGHTING FACT

Most of the more than 3 million Civil War soldiers were civilians who volunteered for military service. The majority were farmers, but there were also blacksmiths, lawyers, dentists, and others.

conjoined twins—twins who are born with their bodies joined together in some way

civilian—a person who is not in the military

CHAPTER TWO

EQUIPMENT AND TECHNOLOGY

Changing equipment and technology, from horses and ships to rifles and medical supplies, had a huge effect on how the Civil War was waged.

THE DANGERS OF BEING A GENERAL

Unlike modern commanders, Civil War generals fought right alongside their soldiers. Because they were often on horseback while their men were on foot, generals were easy to spot. That's a reason why they were 50 percent more likely to die than regular soldiers. Their horses were in danger too. Union General George Custer had 11 horses shot from under him. Confederate General Nathan Bedford Forrest lost 29 horses.

General Benjamin Harrison →

FOUR-LEGGED WAR HEROES

Horses carried soldiers and messengers, pulled heavy guns, and carried supplies. They were heroes of the Civil War. The North had 3.4 million steeds, while the South had 1.7 million. Confederate **cavalry** units were formed by rich men who brought their own horses.

Up to 1.5 million horses died in the war, but not all lost their lives in battle. Most horses died of disease and starvation and lived a life of just seven months on average. The most famous Civil War horse was Traveller, who belonged to Robert E. Lee. Traveller lived through the entire war.

↓ General Robert E. Lee and Traveller

cavalry—soldiers who travel and fight on horseback

RIFLES

Rifles ranked as the most important weapons in the Civil War. Rifles were different from the muskets used in the Revolutionary War, the War of 1812, and the Mexican-American War. Muskets only fired one round at a time. Some new rifles at the time were "repeating" weapons that could fire up to seven shots without reloading. While muskets were loaded from the front, some newer rifles could be loaded near the trigger. Rifles had greater range than muskets. Rifles could accurately hit a target 200 to 300 yards away. The range for a musket was only about 50 yards.

Civil War rifle →

← Civil War bullet

FIGHTING FACT

At the Battle of Wilson's Creek in Missouri, one Union bullet and one Confederate bullet met in mid-flight and fused together. They were found on the battlefield in the 1950s.

Rifles got their name because of their "rifled" barrels, or barrels with grooves. The barrels of rifles had grooves that made the bullets spin, which meant greater accuracy. Civil War rifles used bullets called Minié balls that were long and pointed at one end while musket shot was round.

Rifle specialists trained to hit targets at long distances were called sharpshooters. There were special units of sharpshooters on both sides.

Rifle specialists

↓ USS Baron DeKalb

A NEW KIND OF SHIP

Ironclads, ships with outer hulls made of iron or steel, became important tools in the Civil War. At first neither side had an ironclad warship. The Confederates took wooden warships and covered them with metal. Then they built real ironclad ships from the bottom up. A Union spy soon discovered what the southerners were doing. The North, then, hurried to build its own ironclads. It successfully used ironclads to **blockade** the South and stop southerners from getting supplies from other countries.

LOST AND FOUND

To stop the northern blockade, Confederates needed a secret weapon against ships. Confederates built a submarine called the Hunley. These subs were dangerous and **unreliable**, but the South was desperate. Although 13 men were killed in tests, Confederates used the Hunley to attack the USS *Housatonic*. The attack was successful, but the sub sank in the harbor. It was found about 140 years later, in 1995, with its commander and all eight crew still at their posts.

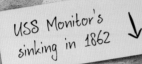

USS Monitor's sinking in 1862 ↓

blockade—to close off an area to keep people or supplies from going in or out

unreliable—not to be depended on

MEDICAL TREATMENT

More soldiers died of disease in the Civil War than in battle. One reason is that doctors didn't know much about germs. They didn't wash their hands after treating a patient's wounds to protect the next patient.

Doctors performed a lot of **amputations** to avoid infected wounds. They got so good at it that they were nicknamed "sawbones." Doctors used painkillers for surgery, but antibiotics used to kill germs were not invented yet.

More than one million Union soldiers got malaria, a disease spread by mosquitoes. Mosquitoes thrived in the hot, wet southern climate. But the number one killer during the war was **dysentery**. Soldiers got dysentery because they didn't take showers or wash their clothes. They ate from dirty dishes and drank polluted water. Soldiers also suffered from typhoid fever, yellow fever, swamp fever, smallpox, pneumonia, and tuberculosis.

One common medicine during the Civil War was calomel, made with mercury. Doctors used it to treat many different illnesses. Union Surgeon General William A. Hammond warned that mercury was poison. He was dismissed from his post for refusing to order it for army hospitals. Years later, doctors agreed that Hammond was right.

↓ Union Army hospital

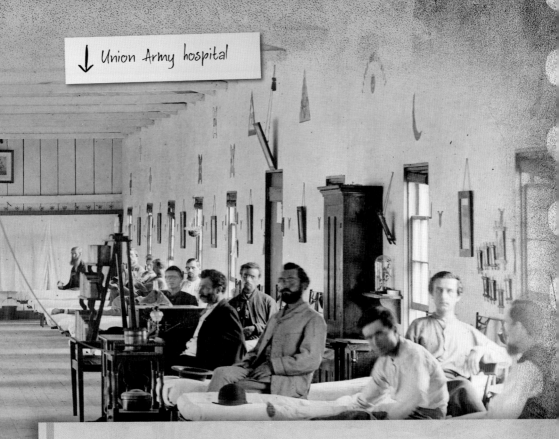

amputation—the removal of a body part such as an arm or a leg

dysentery—infection of the intestines resulting in severe diarrhea

BATTLE STORIES

The battlefields were where many of the most compelling stories of the Civil War happened. From the Battle of Shiloh to the Battle of Gettysburg, many Civil War secrets can be found in the very ground.

↓ Battle of Shiloh

FIGHTING FACT

When the Civil War started, there was no no such thing as an ambulance. Some wounded soldiers lay on the battlefield for days. As the need to remove these men from the battlefield grew, horse-drawn wagons were finally designed to carry them away.

BATTLE OF SHILOH APRIL 6-7, 1862

Injured soldiers lay in the mud for days after the Battle of Shiloh in Tennessee. Normally they would have died of infection in their wounds. Instead, they noticed a strange, unnatural glow coming from their wounds at night. They called it "Angel's Glow." When the soldiers finally got to a hospital, doctors noticed that the patients with glowing wounds were healing.

Nobody knew why until two high school students from Maryland did a science project in 2001. The students learned that the glow was produced by "good" **bacteria** called *Panellus stipticus*, which glows in the dark. The bacteria come from insects. It doesn't usually live in humans because people's body temperatures are too high. The bodies of the soldiers in the mud at Shiloh got very cold at night. The Angel's Glow fought off the bad bacteria in their wounds and kept the soldiers alive.

Panellus stipticus ↗

bacteria—very small living things that exist everywhere in nature

BATTLE OF ANTIETAM SEPTEMBER 17, 1862

Confederate troops had captured some Union uniforms at Harper's Ferry, just before the Battle of Antietam in Maryland. Wearing the blue uniforms they had captured, the Confederates made a surprise attack at Antietam. The Union soldiers were confused because men wearing their own uniforms were attacking. The Union soldiers held their fire, which was a big mistake. Even Robert E. Lee, the Confederate general, wasn't sure which soldiers were his until he saw the Confederate battle flag flying over his troops. Union forces **retreated**.

FIGHTING FACT

At Antietam, Nurse Clara Barton was working so close to the fighting that a bullet whizzed through her sleeve. It killed the man she was treating.

Siege of Vicksburg

SIEGE OF VICKSBURG MAY TO JULY 1863

In the spring of 1863, Confederates hid in Vicksburg, Mississippi, a town on a bluff overlooking the Mississippi River. If the North captured Vicksburg, it could cut the Confederate states in half and control river traffic. The Union army attacked the town again and again for 47 days. At last, the Confederates surrendered on July 4, 1863. Vicksburg refused to celebrate the United States' Independence Day on the Fourth of July 4 for 81 years after the surrender.

retreat—to move back or withdraw from a difficult situation

BATTLE OF GETTYSBURG JULY 1-3, 1863

The Battle of Gettysburg in Pennsylvania was the bloodiest clash of the war. A total of 7,058 died, 33,264 were wounded, and 10,790 went missing. Soldiers of the First Minnesota unit captured the battle flag of the 28th Virginia regiment. Many Civil War battle flags were given back to their original units after the war. But when Virginia asked Minnesota to give this flag back in 2013, the answer was no. The governor of Minnesota said the flag was earned with the blood of soldiers from his state.

Battle of Gettysburg

Battle of Chickamauga →

BATTLE OF CHICKAMAUGA
SEPTEMBER 18-20, 1863

As darkness fell, soldiers from the 21st Ohio Infantry saw some men coming toward them but couldn't tell if they were friend or foe. When the soldiers asked which side the men were on, several voices answered, "We're Jeff Davis' boys."

The Union troops thought they meant Union General Jefferson C. Davis, so they held their fire. Wrong! They meant Confederate President Jefferson F. Davis. The Ohioans were captured by Confederate soldiers from the 7th Florida Infantry.

MORE SECRETS

More surprising stories of the Civil War may still come to light. Most of the war's battles were fought in the South. Letters and artifacts hidden in older homes in the South may be waiting to be discovered. The Civil War is bound to reveal even more secrets, one by one.

THE BLOODIEST WAR

Soldiers fighting in the Civil War numbered 3.5 million. More than 600,000 of them died or were wounded in battle. More soldiers died in the Civil War than in any other war the United States has ever fought. In terms of the number of people who were killed or wounded, the Civil War is the bloodiest war in United States history.

a depiction of the South's surrender to the North at Appomattox Courthouse

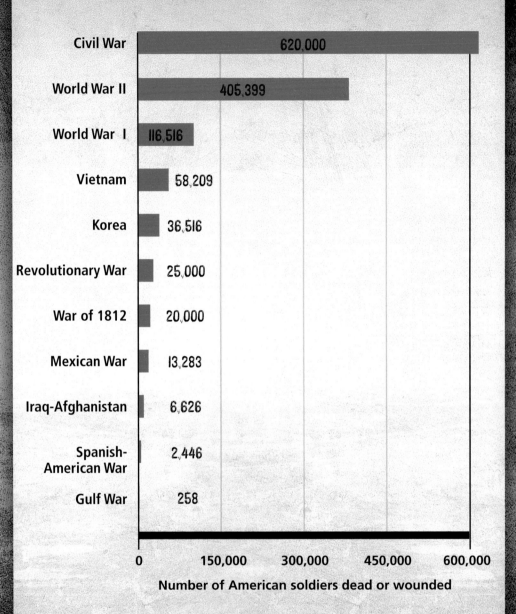

Civil War Devastation: A War Comparison

War	Number of American soldiers dead or wounded
Civil War	620,000
World War II	405,399
World War I	116,516
Vietnam	58,209
Korea	36,516
Revolutionary War	25,000
War of 1812	20,000
Mexican War	13,283
Iraq-Afghanistan	6,626
Spanish-American War	2,446
Gulf War	258

Number of American soldiers dead or wounded

NOTE: The numbers given represent the number of soldiers who died in battle plus the number of wounded soldiers. War records, especially older war records, are often difficult to accurately confirm, but these statistic are a fair approximation.

GLOSSARY

amputation (am-pyuh-TAY shun)—the removal of a body part such as an arm or a leg

bacteria (bak-TEER-ee-ah)—very small living things that exist everywhere in nature

blockade (blok-AYD)—to close off of an area to keep people or supplies from going in or out

cavalry (KA-vuhl-ree)—soldiers who travel and fight on horseback

civilian (si-VIL-yuhn)—a person who is not in the military

Confederacy (kuhn-FE-druh-see)—the southern states that fought against the northern states in the Civil War; also called the Confederate States of America

conjoined twins (kun-JOYND TWINZ)—twins who are born with their bodies joined together in some way

immigrant (IM-uh-gruhnt)—a person who comes to live in a different country than the one in which they were born

pension (PEN-shun)—money the government sends to retired people

retreat (ri-TREET)—to move back or withdraw from a difficult situation

Union (YOON-yun)—the United States of America; also the northern states that fought against the southern states in the Civil War

unreliable (un-re-LYE-uh-buhl)—not to be depended on

CRITICAL THINKING USING THE COMMON CORE

1. On page 15, horses are mentioned as war heroes. Do you think it was right to use animals in war? Why or why not? (Key Ideas and Details)

2. Some of the Civil War's secrets were found in letters or artifacts that were discovered many years after the war. What kinds of secrets about the Civil War might still be revealed, if you were to guess? (Key Ideas and Details)

READ MORE

Fitzgerald, Stephanie. *A Civil War Timeline.* War Timelines. North Mankato, Minn.: Capstone Press, 2014.

Fitzgerald, Stephanie. *The Split History of the Battle of Gettysburg: A Perspectives Flip Book.* Perspectives Flip Books. North Mankato, Minn.: Capstone Press, 2013.

Fitzgerald, Stephanie. *The Split History of the Civil War: A Perspectives Flip Book.* Perspectives Flip Books. North Mankato, Minn.: Capstone Press, 2012.

INTERNET SITES

FactHound offers a safe, fun way to find Internet sites related to this book. All of the sites on FactHound have been researched by our staff. Here's all you do:

Visit *www.facthound.com*

FactHound will fetch the best sites for you!

Type in this code: **9781545741381**

Check out projects, games and lots more at
www.capstonekids.com

INDEX